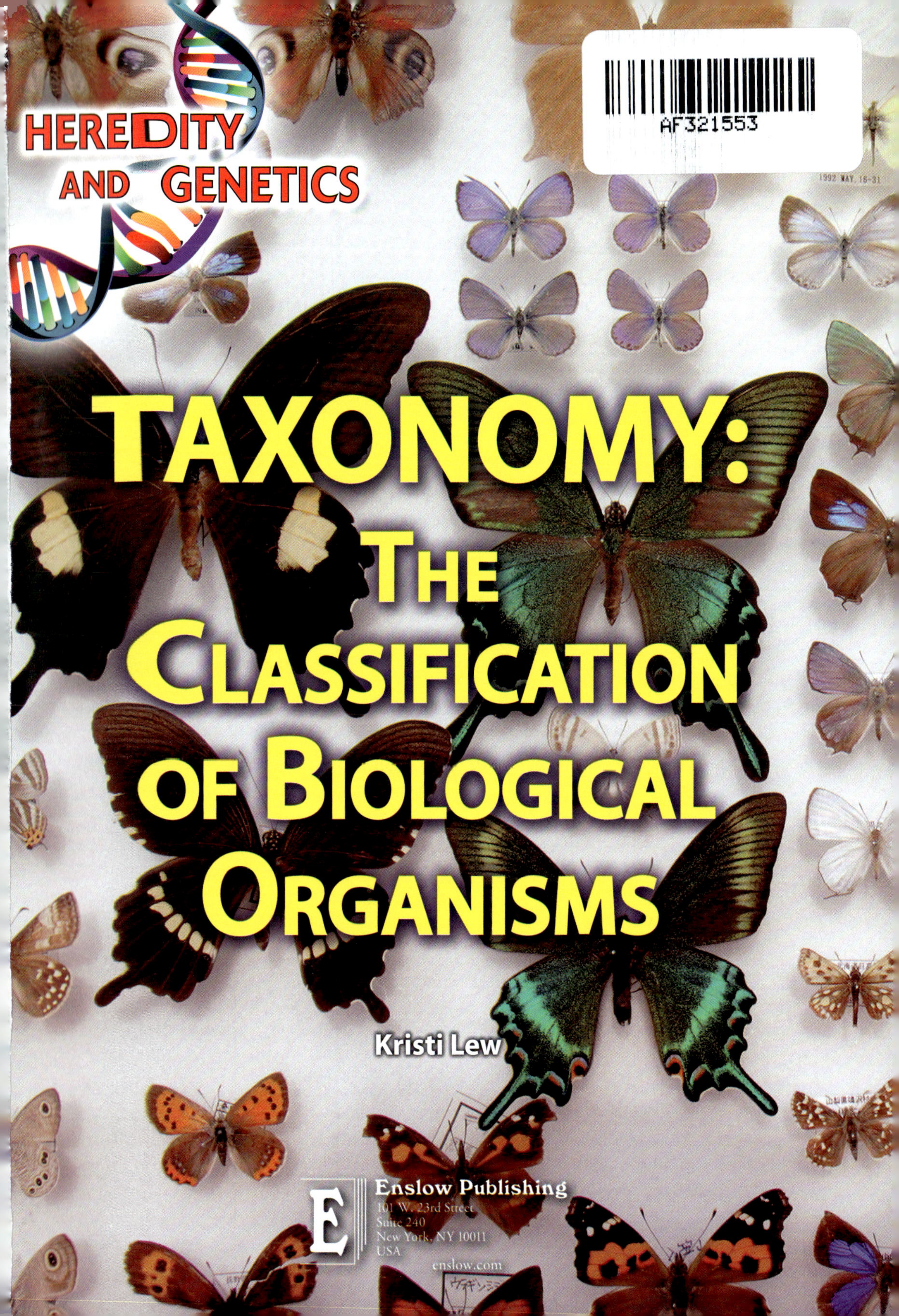

HEREDITY AND GENETICS
AF321553
TAXONOMY:
THE CLASSIFICATION OF BIOLOGICAL ORGANISMS
Kristi Lew
Enslow Publishing
101 W. 23rd Street
Suite 240
New York, NY 10011
USA
enslow.com

Published in 2019 by Enslow Publishing, LLC
101 W. 23rd Street, Suite 240, New York, NY 10011

Library of Congress Cataloging-in-Publication Data

Names: Lew, Kristi, author.
Title: Taxonomy : the classification of biological organisms / Kristi Lew.
Description: New York : Enslow, [2019] | Series: Heredity and genetics | Audience: Grade 7-12. | Includes bibliographical references and index.
Identifiers: LCCN 2017056614| ISBN 9780766099388 (library bound) | ISBN 9780766099395 (paperback)
Subjects: LCSH: Biology—Classification—Juvenile literature.
Classification: LCC QH83 .L495 2019 | DDC 578.01/2—dc23
LC record available at https://lccn.loc.gov/2017056614

Printed in the United States of America

To Our Readers: We have done our best to make sure all websites in this book were active and appropriate when we went to press. However, the author and the publisher have no control over and assume no liability for the material available on those websites or on any websites they may link to. Any comments or suggestions can be sent by email to customerservice@enslow.com.

Portions of this book originally appeared in *Classification of Living Organisms* by Mark J. Lewis.

Photo Credits: Cover, p. 1 Paul Atkinson/Shutterstock.com; p. 4 D K Grove/Shutterstock.com; p. 8 Chinese School/Societe Asiatique, College de France, Paris, France/Archives Charmet/ Bridgeman Images; p. 10 MidoSemsem/Shutterstock.com; p. 12 (top) Miles Away Photography/ Shutterstock.com; p. 12 (bottom) Palomba/Shutterstock.com; p. 14 AF Fotografie/Alamy Stock Photo; pp. 19, 39 Hulton Archive/Getty Images; p. 20 Monica Schroeder/Science Source; p. 22 Georgios Kollidas/Shutterstock.com; p. 27 Corbis Historical/Getty Images; p. 31 mhgstan/Shutterstock.com; p. 33 (left) vladsilver/Shutterstock.com; p. 33 (right) Ondrej Prosicky/Shutterstock.com; p. 34 Dorling Kindersley/Getty Images; p. 35 (top) dioch/Shutterstock.com; p. 35 (bottom) orin/Shutterstock.com; p. 36 Trum Ronnarong/Shutterstock.com; p. 37 Frank Greenaway/Dorling Kindersley/Getty Images; p. 42 Universal Images Group/Getty Images; p. 44 Spencer Sutton/ Science Source; p. 47 (top) Manamana/Shutterstock.com; p. 47 (bottom) wildestanimal/Shutterstock.com; p. 51 (top) piya saisawatdikul/Shutterstock.com; p. 51 (bottom) Brian Lasenby/Shutterstock.com; p. 52 Gwen Shockey/Science Source; p. 56 (top) Sergey Uryadnikov/Shutterstock.com; p. 56 (bottom) Kiki Dohmeier/Shutterstock.com; p. 59 Lebendkulturen.de/Shutterstock.com; p. 61 Oguz Aral/Shutterstock.com; p. 63 natasha53/Shutterstock.com; p. 65 Designua/Shutterstock.com; p. 68 Nicole Helgason/Shutterstock.com; interior page headers Juli Hansen/Shutterstock.com (DNA strand); interior page backgrounds and back cover paulista/Shutterstock.com (DNA double helix).

Contents

Bookstore owners usually shelve books with similar topics together. Categorizing books in this fashion helps people find the books they are looking for. Similarly, living organisms are grouped together to make them easier to study.

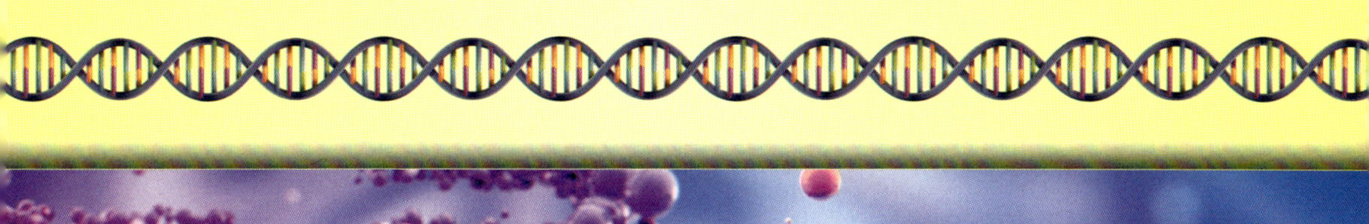

Introduction

Planet Earth is home to an amazing variety of life forms. Scientists do not always agree on exactly how many species exist on Earth. Some studies estimate there are less than two million. Others suggest more than one trillion different species currently exist or have existed in the past. What is certain is that, to date, scientists have named and described only a small fraction of the numerous plant and animal species. With so many living things to identify, and new organisms being discovered all the time, scientists need a systematic approach to organize the assortment of living things on Earth.

Imagine, for example, a library in which all the books—mysteries, biographies, science fiction novels, encyclopedias, and all the rest—are scattered about randomly. Some of the books are downstairs, some are upstairs, some are in closets, and some are in a back storeroom. How can people find the books they are looking for in such a disorganized space? How might a librarian organize the books so people can find them easily? The librarian could arrange the books by color. In a library organized by color, all the red books would be grouped together, all the black books would be in the same place, and all the green books, regardless of subject, would be on the same shelf. One book that someone needs to research a subject might be red, but the rest of the books on that subject might be with the black books or across the building with the green books. This system would not make finding a book easy. Perhaps color would not be the best method of classification. Size might work, but again, some science books might be with the large encyclopedias while others would be on another shelf with the paperback novels. Why not just group all the biographies together, all the science books together, and all the novels together? Of course, that is what libraries do—they group books by subject—so people can find what they need.

Once all the science books have been grouped together, there are still numerous ways in which to sort them. How should the books be categorized? Should they be grouped by author? Or broken down by subject? Each classification scheme has its advantages and disadvantages. Grouping living organisms is very similar. Unlike library books, which come with summaries to describe what they are all about, however, new species can be a bit more difficult to organize.

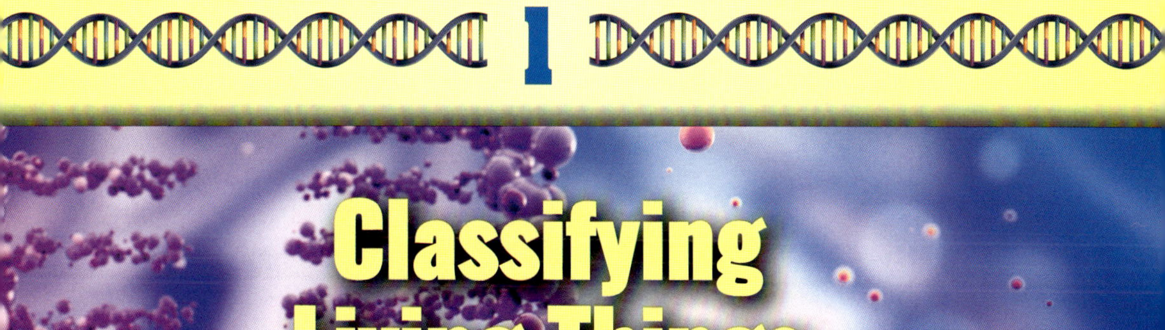

Taxonomy is the science of classification. Scientists describe, name, and group organisms based on a standardized system. Imagine trying to find an item in a grocery store that did not label their products. Or, worse yet, labeled them incorrectly. How would someone know if a particular box contained cake mix or laundry detergent? If the box contains laundry detergent, dessert is not going to turn out well. Like grocery store labels, taxonomy gives scientists a way to communicate information about living things in a reliable way.

Early Classification

People have been trying to classify living organisms throughout history. Oral tradition suggests that, as early as 3000 BCE, Shen Nung, legendary emperor of China, may have tested hundreds of herbs as potential medicines. Collected writings credited to him describe 365 drugs and medical preparations made from living things and minerals. The Ebers Papyrus, which dates to 1550 BCE, shows that plants were used for their medicinal properties in ancient Egypt. A cursive form of hieroglyphics, called hieratic script, was used to name the plants and describe their properties.

The mythological emperor Shen Nung reportedly tasted hundreds of herbs before dying of a toxic overdose. He is often called the Father of Chinese Medicine.

The first person to create a system of rules to classify living organisms was a Greek scientist and philosopher named Aristotle (384–322 BCE). Aristotle pointed out that classification requires two steps. First, organisms have to be carefully described. Think back to the library and grocery store. One way to classify items is by subject or function. But before librarians and store owners can put a book or an item on a shelf or in an aisle, they need to identify and describe the subject or function of the item. Describing the function of a store item is easy because it comes in a package that specifies that information. Describing a newly discovered species is not so simple. A scientist must gather data by measuring the new life-form and, possibly, dissecting it. He or she would also observe the organism's behaviors and its habitat. This gathered information helps the scientist determine if the lifeform really is a newly discovered species or if it is just a variation on one that has already been described.

Aristotle pointed out that observations are not enough. Traits or features must also be carefully compared with the traits of similar organisms. Behavior, color, and habitat were features that were often used to classify animals. But some classifications are more complicated. Killer whales and great white sharks, for example, both live in the ocean. They are both swimmers. Each animal also has a dorsal fin than helps keep the animal upright in the water. Both creatures are predators. Are they closely related? Actually, no. Aristotle pointed out that only some characteristics were appropriate for use in classification.

Consider the following: many kinds of animals have two eyes. Lots of aquatic animals have fins. Many different kinds of animals are predators. These traits are not reliable for classification purposes. Aristotle worked to find more reliable traits to categorize living organisms. Does the animal lay eggs, like birds,

Aristotle is thought to have created
the first classification system for
living organisms.

fish, and reptiles? Or does the animal give birth to live young, like mammals? Is the animal cold-blooded, as reptiles and fish are, or warm-blooded like mammals and birds? Does the animal breathe using gills or lungs? These traits proved to be far more reliable for classification. For example, the great white shark produces eggs, which it holds inside its body, while the killer whale gives birth to a well-developed baby whale. The great white has a body temperature that is the same as the ocean around it. The killer whale maintains a steady body temperature of ninety-nine degrees Fahrenheit (thirty-seven degrees Celsius). It has blubber to insulate itself from the cold ocean water. The great white breathes using gills. Gills extract oxygen directly from the water so the shark never needs to surface. The killer whale uses lungs to breathe, just as humans do. It must surface to take giant breaths. It can then hold its breath for as long as fifteen minutes! Using Aristotle's early system, it becomes clear that although both whales and sharks swim, and have similar colors and shapes, they are not as closely related as whales and people are—even though humans don't live in the water.

Aristotle did not always get it right. One of his early classification missteps was his attempt to classify animals by how they moved. He saw three distinct groups: animals that fly, animals that swim, and animals that walk. Birds fly, fish swim, and humans walk. The main problem with this system quickly becomes apparent when one considers ducks. Many types of ducks spend most of their lives swimming. But they are not fish. These feathered, egg-laying creatures are clearly related to hawks, which rarely swim, and ostriches, which cannot fly. Are there any other problems in using this method? How about in the case of an alligator? This creature has scales like the fish and does live much of its life in the water. But it breathes air and lays eggs, as a

Killer whales (*top*) and great white sharks (*bottom*) both live in the sea, but killer whales are mammals and more closely related to humans than to sharks, which are fish.

bird does. No fish has lungs. The alligator can live out of the water unlike fish. This system of using movement as a characteristic for classification was not successful in categorizing life on Earth.

The Great Chain of Being

Aristotle did try to put living things in order. His system of classification was called the *Scala Naturae* in Latin, which in English translates to the "great chain of being." Aristotle saw living things in order from lowest to highest. Because he saw the universe as perfect, the chain was perfect. Each organism supposedly sat just below another more complex organism in perfect order with simple plants at the bottom and humans at the top. Aristotle also saw the universe as unchanging. In his world, species did not change over time.

This idea of a chain organized from simple to complex was not a problem for classifying some creatures. A human is higher on the chain than a flea. It was, however, very difficult to explain exactly what "higher on the chain" meant. Did it mean "more intelligent than?" Or "more powerful than? " Or "morally superior to? " And what is superior—an oak or a maple? A dog or a cat? Aristotle had a hard time coming up with a set of rules to solve this problem. The chain provided no clear solution for these questions. The other problem with this model was that it was not evolutionary. Aristotle saw life on Earth to be unchanging but this notion made it very difficult to explain certain missing links in the chain. However, his idea was very important because it was perhaps the first attempt to put living organisms in order.

Aristotle and other early classifiers of life brought some order to the thousands of living things around them. They did this for two reasons. First, people were interested in plant and animal substances for their medical uses. Second, as a scientist

This 1597 engraving from a religious book is based off Aristotle's "great chain of being," an attempt to place living things in hierarchal order. From top to bottom sits God, angels, humans, animals, plants, minerals, and lastly the Devil and demons.

AN INTELLECTUAL POWERHOUSE

Taxonomy was not Aristotle's only interest or contribution to science and society. His intellectual range covered most sciences, including biology, chemistry, and physics. But he was interested in ethics, history, metaphysics, poetry, and political theory, as well. He was also incredibly influential in developing the fields of philosophy and formal logic. Aristotle did not invent logical thinking, but he was the first person to write down ideas and rules that described what made a line of reason logical. Logical reasoning is a way of thinking about or examining something according to a set of strict rational principles. Scientists use logic to uncover facts that can be backed up with evidence.

and philosopher, Aristotle was very curious. He simply wanted to figure out how things were related. Aristotle's contributions were particularly important because he created a standard system of naming and because he showed that the classification of living things requires two steps: the thorough description of each organism, and the thoughtful comparison of similar organisms. He was also the first to try to put all living organisms in order. Though not all of his ideas were factually correct, they have influenced the way people look at living things for more than two thousand years.

After Aristotle's death, much of his classification work was forgotten in the West. A great deal of it was lost or accidentally destroyed. In the ninth and tenth centuries, however, Arab and Persian scholars translated the writings of Aristotle and studied them. Through these scholars' writings, the works of Aristotle were reintroduced to people in the West. Because of their scholarship, Aristotle's work became the foundation of medieval philosophy, theology, and natural science.

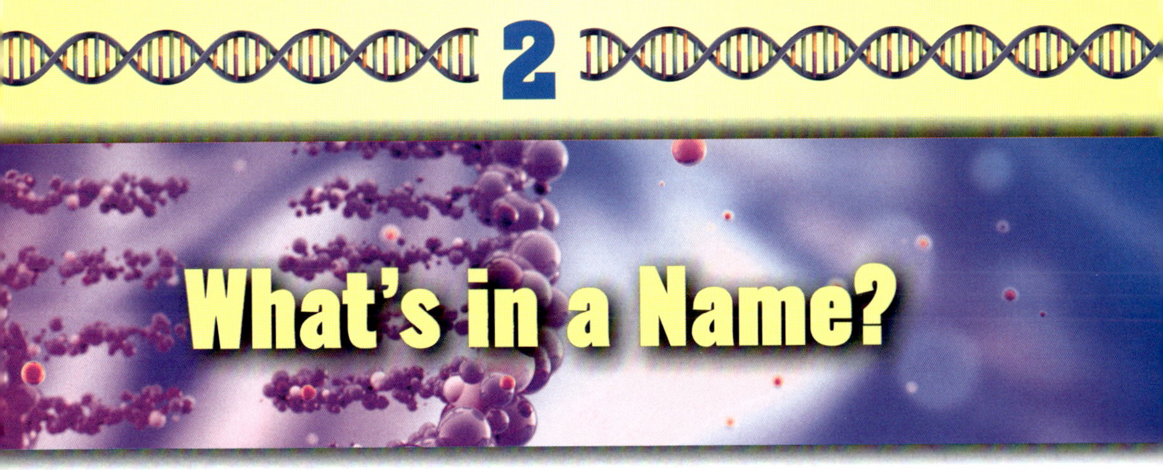

Naming new organisms was a major problem throughout the history of classification. People had described living things for thousands of years but there was no common system of naming them. Often, they were just given names that described where they were found, like "flower of the river." The same organism might have twenty different names, which led to confusion. Aristotle put similar animals into groups called genera (plural for genus). It was a general category for any creatures Aristotle saw as being similar. Then he further divided the genera into different species.

The First Taxonomists

In the late 1500s, there was a renewed interest in describing the natural world. Unlike today, Renaissance scholars were frequently experts in several different fields of research. Many doctors were also botanists because plants were often used to treat illnesses. Andrea Cesalpino (1519–1603) was a doctor and botanist living in Italy during the sixteenth century. Cesalpino studied Aristotle's approach to classifying organisms. He used Aristotle's work to come up with his own classification method. Cesalpino is often called the first taxonomist because he used a logical approach to classification. Cesalpino carefully analyzed and compared all the plants he knew before selecting the characteristics he used to divide them into groups. Cesalpino classified more than fifteen hundred plants in one of his publications. He decided that seeds and seedlings were important characteristics to consider when dividing plant groups.

Two Swiss brothers, Gaspard and Johann Bauhin, followed up on Cesalpino's work. In 1623 they published *Pinax theatri botanici* (Illustrated Exposition of Plants), a book that listed more than six thousand species of plants. The Bauhins grouped plants by genus and tried to keep the species names as short as possible. The book also helped clear up some of the confusion caused by repeated naming of plants.

One of the most significant scientists working on classification at that time was John Ray (1627–1705), an English scholar and naturalist. Ray was an ordained Anglican priest and he sought to uncover "God's natural order" by classifying organisms.

Ray looked at the idea of species differently from that of most scientists of his era. Most botanists focused on one or two characters when classifying plants. Ray looked at the total morphology, or the form and structure of the whole plant. He influenced other botanists to start looking at the total morphology, too. Ray also noticed that plants could be divided into two large groups based on their number of cotyledons. Cotyledons are leaf-like parts of the plant embryo that serve as storage organs for nutrients. If a plant's seed contained one cotyledon, Ray called that plant a monocot. If a plant's seed contained two cotyledons, Ray called that plant a dicot. While monocots and dicots are still recognized as subclasses of plants in some classification systems, these seemingly simple divisions turned out to not be as clear as Ray believed.

Andrea Cesalpino carefully analyzed the plants he studied and placed them into groups based on their shared characteristics.

Besides his extensive work with plants, Ray also was one of the first scientists to promote the idea of fossils as forms of dead organisms. He did not, however, believe that God would let living things go extinct. Instead, Ray considered dinosaur fossils to be animals that had not yet been discovered. He simply thought that they lived in some other part of the world. Toward the end of his life, Ray began to ask more questions about fossils and to wonder if Earth was actually older than traditional theology taught.

The Father of Taxonomy

In this flurry of work by numerous scientists with widely varying systems of classification, the work of one Swedish botanist stands

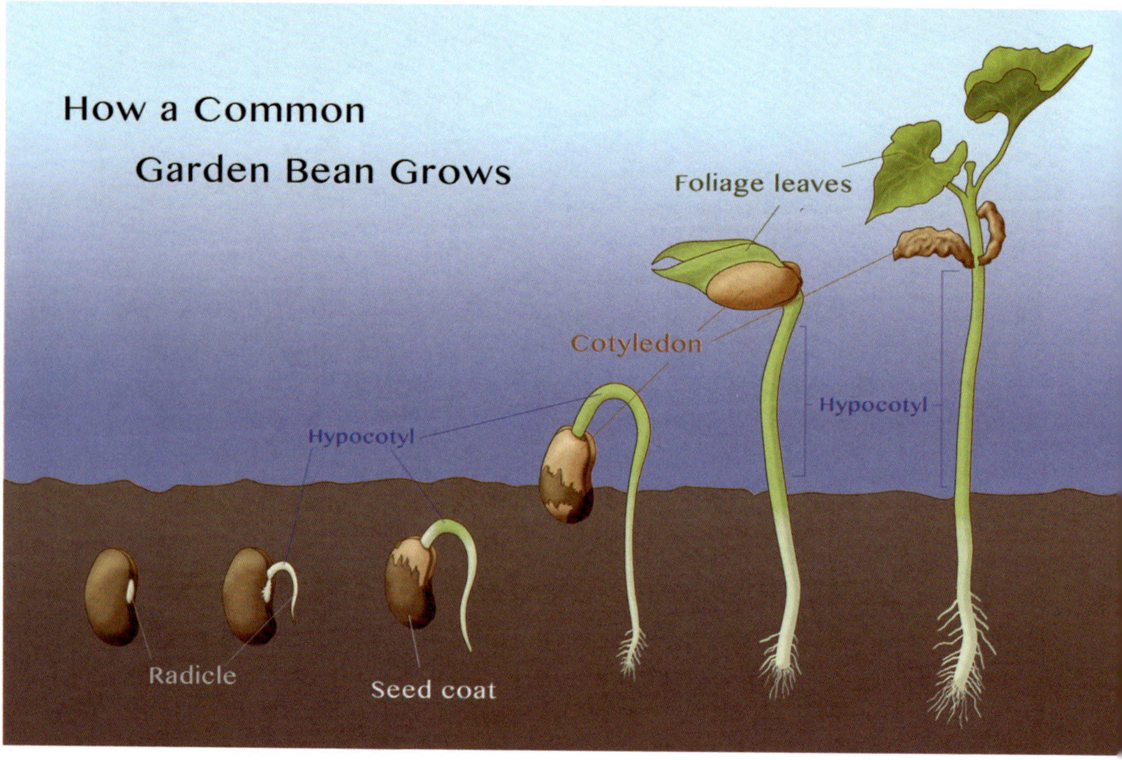

The number of cotyledons present is one of the characteristics botanists have used to classify plants into different groups.

out. Carl Linnaeus (also known as Carl von Linné) was born in 1707. Like many noted taxonomists of his time, Linnaeus spent his childhood fascinated with plants. His father taught him the names of all the plants in their garden. When Linnaeus went to school he often skipped class to look for plants in the countryside. Linnaeus's classmates nicknamed him "little botanist."

Linnaeus's parents wanted him to become a priest. However, Linnaeus showed little interest or talent for the subjects studied by priests. There was a doctor who taught at Linnaeus's high school, who was impressed by Linnaeus's knowledge of plants. He convinced Linnaeus's father that Linnaeus should study medicine so he would be able to use his knowledge of plants in his career.

Linnaeus became a doctor and respected naturalist. He studied plants, animals, and minerals. He also thought a lot about how to best classify organisms. The problem with classification at Linnaeus's time was there were far too many systems of organization. People often gave plants long Latin names that described the plant. For example, a plant may have been called "the red flower that grows by water." Linnaeus saw this as confusing and cumbersome. He did two things to help clarify this.

A Two-Part Name

Linnaeus reduced his names for organisms to two parts. In 1753 he published a plant book that introduced his binomial nomenclature method of naming organisms. He was not the first person to give organisms two names, but he was the first to consistently use a system that only used two names. Linnaeus applied some of the genus names created by the Bauhin brothers for the first name that is used to describe a whole group of similar organisms. The second name in Linnaeus's system was a one-word species name. Sometimes Linnaeus took a word from descriptive names that

Carl Linnaeus developed a consistent method for naming organisms. His system, called binomial nomenclature, is still in use today.

other people had already given to the plant. Sometimes he made up his own. Linnaeus was the first person to use species names that did not always describe the plant. He sometimes named plants after people he knew. For example, a friend and fellow botanist, Elias Tillandz, disliked traveling by boat. Linnaeus named a genus of plants that does not grow well in damp soil *Tillandsia*, after his friend. He also named a small weed *Sigesbeckia orientalis* after his rival and critic, botanist Johann Siegesbeck.

Many species named during Linnaeus's time still have the same name today. Scientists still use Linnaeus's binominal system to give newly discovered species a name. The genus name together with the species name for an organism is called its scientific name. As in Linnaeus's time, scientific names for new species are still created using Latin or Greek words. Latin is more commonly used than Greek so the scientific name for an organism is sometimes referred to as its Latin name. Scientific names are always italicized. The species name often describes a notable characteristic of the organism. For example, all maple trees belong to the genus *Acer*. *Acer* means hard or sharp in Latin and it refers to the sharp points on the leaves of most maples. The scientific name for sugar maples is *Acer saccharinum*. The sweet sap of sugar maples is used to make maple syrup. *Saccharinum* means "sugar" or "sweet" in Latin.

Species Naming Today

Like Linnaeus, today's scientists are still discovering and re-naming species. In 2005 the genus of *Acacia* trees and shrubs was split into three different genera by botanists. Australian botanists waged a campaign to allow the Australian species to keep the name *Acacia*. *Acacia* species make up a large percentage of wild and commercially grown plant species in Australia. The botanists

PLAYING THE NAME GAME

The translation of a scientific name will usually reveal information about an organism but, occasionally, it also reveals the sense of humor of the scientists who named it. The scientific name for broccoli, for example, is *Brassica oleracea*, which literally means "cabbage, smelly." A genus of small sea snails was named *Bittium* in 1847. So what were scientists to do when they found a group of even tinier sea snails? Create a new genus called *Ittibittium*, of course! Other whimsical scientific names include a genus of mites called *Darthvaderum*, a Fijian snail called *Ba humbui*, and a clam called *Abra cadabra*. In 2009 scientists named a diving beetle they discovered in Venezuela after the comedian Stephen Colbert. The beetle's scientific name is *Agaporomorphus colberti*.

successfully argued that changing the scientific names of the almost one thousand *Acacia* species in Australia would confuse people, hurt the horticulture industry, and require many plant publications to be rewritten. Australian *Acacia* trees, such as *Acacia decora,* were allowed to keep their name. African, Asian, and American acacias now have the new generic names *Vachellia* and *Senegalia*.

When a new species is discovered or an old species is renamed, the name for the new species must meet the requirements of an international organization. If it is a plant, the name is approved by the International Congress on Code of Botanical Nomenclature.

New animal species names are approved by the International Commission on Zoological Nomenclature. New bacterial species are approved by the International Code of Nomenclature of Bacteria.

The requirements for naming species differ from organization to organization, but the major requirements are the same. It is important, of course, not to repeat names that have already been used. It is also important that just like the kingdom, the phylum, the class, the order, and the family, both the genus and species are written in Latin. People of all nations and languages use scientific names and Latin is currently a language that no nation calls its own, so it is seen as a neutral language.

The species name must also follow the binomial naming system that has been used now for hundreds of years. Each name must have a genus and a specific epithet, or specific name. The genus is capitalized while the specific epithet is not. Both parts of the name must be italicized. One example is the scientific name of humans: *Homo sapiens*. The genus is *Homo*. The specific name is *sapiens*. The two parts together are the species name.

3

Grouping Organisms

In addition to his binomial naming system, Linnaeus also introduced a hierarchical system of organization. A hierarchy is an arrangement that divides large groups into smaller groups. The small groups can be placed in order beneath the title of the big group. For example, a high school has a hierarchical order. All students at the school are high school students. Within that large group of students, the students can be divided into seniors, juniors, sophomores, and freshmen. They can then be further divided into homerooms. But just like Linnaeus's system, the smaller groups have to fit neatly into the larger groups for the hierarchy to make sense. One organism or student cannot fit into more than one of the larger groups. For example, sports teams would not be a good group to include in a hierarchical diagram of a high school because team members would not all be in the same year of high school and not all students would be on a sports team. Linnaeus's system was a neat hierarchical system.

When Linnaeus was in his late twenties, he published his system for classifying animals and plants in a book called *Systema Naturae* (The System of Nature). The original edition

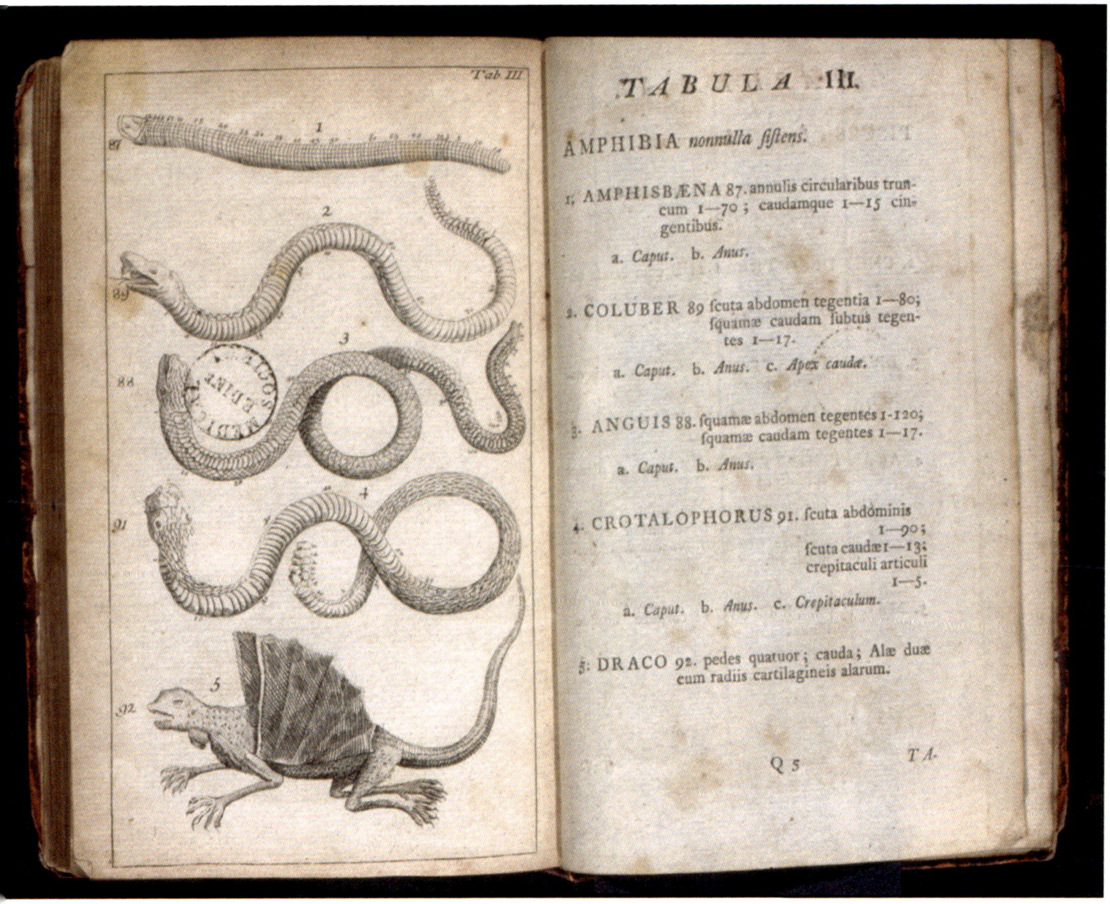

Systema Naturae (1756) contains Linnaeus's drawings and notes identifying different organisms.

DICHOTOMOUS KEYS

Another common tool of classification is called a dichotomous key. A dichotomous key is a series of questions that, based on the answer, separates things into two groups. For example, imagine a tree scientist is hiking through a forest. She comes upon an unfamiliar tree. Her dichotomous tree key asks: "Is the tree growing in the Eastern or the Western United States?" She selects western and is directed to the second half of the book, where western trees are described. From there, she is asked a series of questions such as, "Are the leaves broad or slender?" and "Are the leaves long, like needles, or short and stubby?" By answering the questions, she can successfully narrow down her choices until the identity of the tree is revealed.

of the book was simply an eleven-page list of all discovered plants and animals Linnaeus knew of, classified according to his hierarchical order. His hierarchical order differed from work done previously. Throughout the years, Linnaeus added to his book, which, in its tenth edition in 1758, became a huge two-volume publication.

From Aristotle's time, organisms had been grouped with similar organisms in small groups on the genus level and then into the two very large kingdoms of plants and animals. Linnaeus created more levels in between. He created seven rankings in his hierarchy. Linnaeus's hierarchical ranking started with the very large kingdoms, and went down through phyla (plural for phylum), classes, orders, families, genera, to the smallest unit of classification, species. *System Naturae* was the first classification scheme to group humans with monkeys as primates in the order Primata. Linnaeus's colleagues recognized he had a talent for putting things in order. Unlike Aristotle, Linnaeus did not often run into the problem of finding an organism that fit into more than one of his big categories. The following examples classify the sugar maple, African lion, and human using Linnaeus's system:

	Sugar maple	African lion	Human
Kingdom	Plantae	Animalia	Animalia
Phylum	Magnoliophyta	Chordata	Chordata
Class	Magnoliopsida	Mammalia	Mammalia
Order	Sapindales	Carnivora	Primata
Family	Aceraceae	Felidae	Hominidae
Genus	Acer	Panthera	Homo
Species	Acer saccharum	Panthera leo	Homo sapiens

Over his career, Linnaeus continued to add new species and findings to his *Systema Naturae*. Twelve editions of the book were published before he died. Linnaeus once remarked to a friend that he was upset about all the work he was putting into it. He, like many scientists of his time, simply thought that most living creatures had already been discovered and named! Even today, however, it is widely believed that only a small fraction of the actual living creatures on Earth have been discovered.

Linnaeus's hierarchical system allowed taxonomists of the time to group living organisms based on increasing morphological similarity. Classification systems kept Linnaeus's hierarchy but ignored his classification of plants by flowers. Plant taxonomists preferred John Ray's use of total plant morphology.

Morphology As a Means of Classification

Today scientists do not always use morphology to classify organisms. But morphological similarities can still be used to explain how some organisms are classified. For example, it is easy to see that a northern red oak tree and an emperor penguin are both living organisms. They both grow, change, and reproduce. It is also easy to see that northern red oaks and emperor penguins belong to different kingdoms. The northern red oak is a plant. Plants belong to the kingdom Plantae. A penguin is an animal, so it belongs in the kingdom Animalia.

A monarch butterfly is an animal, too. Penguins and butterflies both have wings but are very different animals. An emperor penguin belongs in the phylum Chordata. All animals in this phylum have three particular structures at some point in their life cycle: a notochord, a hollow dorsal nerve, and pharyngeal slits. These structures do not exist at any time during a monarch butterfly's life cycle. Therefore, the butterfly must belong to a

A monarch butterfly (*Danaus plexippus*) is classified in the kingdom Animalia along with penguins and humans. However, the monarch butterfly belongs to a different phylum because it dos not share the specific characteristics that the other two species have to be classified in Chordata.

different phylum. Indeed, a monarch butterfly belongs to the phylum Arthropoda. Animals in this phylum have segmented bodies and jointed appendages.

An emperor penguin has feathers. Like all birds, the emperor penguin belongs to the class of animals with feathers called Aves. Monarch butterflies have antennae and six pairs of legs so they belong in the Insecta class.

Penguins are funny-looking water birds that stand upright. All penguins belong to the order Sphenisciformes and the family Spheniscidae. All butterflies have a long tube, called a proboscis, that they use to suck nectar. All butterflies belong to the order Lepidoptera. All butterflies that have short front legs that they can't use for walking belong to the Nymphalidae family.

Emperor penguins (*Aptenodytes forsteri*) share the genus *Aptenodytes* with king penguins (*Aptenodytes patagonica*). Emperor and king penguins are larger and somewhat more colorful than other penguins. All butterflies in the *Danaus* genus have orange wings with black veins and white-spotted black margins.

Emperor penguins are taller than king penguins and have a distinct yellow pattern near their ears. One can distinguish a monarch from other similar-looking *Danaus* butterflies by measuring its wings. All monarch butterflies have a wingspan of 3 to 5 inches (7.6 to 12.7 centimeters).

The ranks of Linnaeus's system are one useful method of organizing living things. Except for the rank of species, however, they are arbitrary. That means they have no particular value. There is no definition for the terms "families" or "classes" except to say that one is bigger than another. For example, families fit within a class. Though Linnaeus's contributions would remain important, other methods of classifying living things would soon arise.

Morphological similarities and differences can be used to classify emperor (*left*) and king (*right*) penguins into distinct groupings.

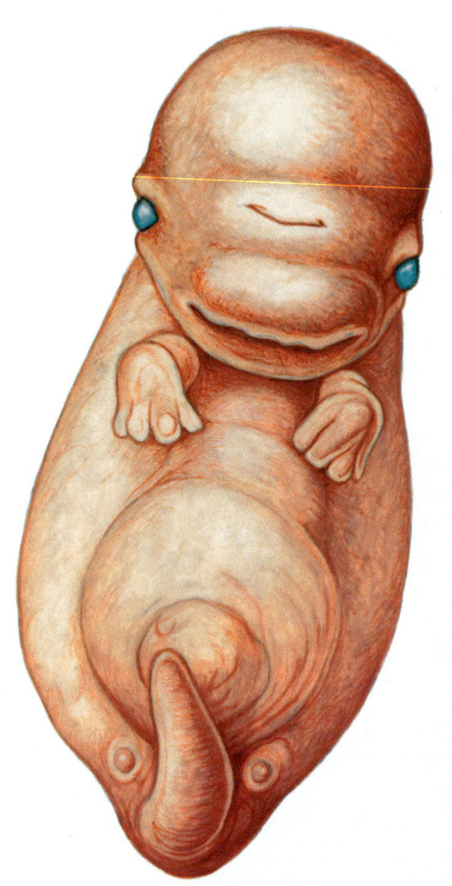
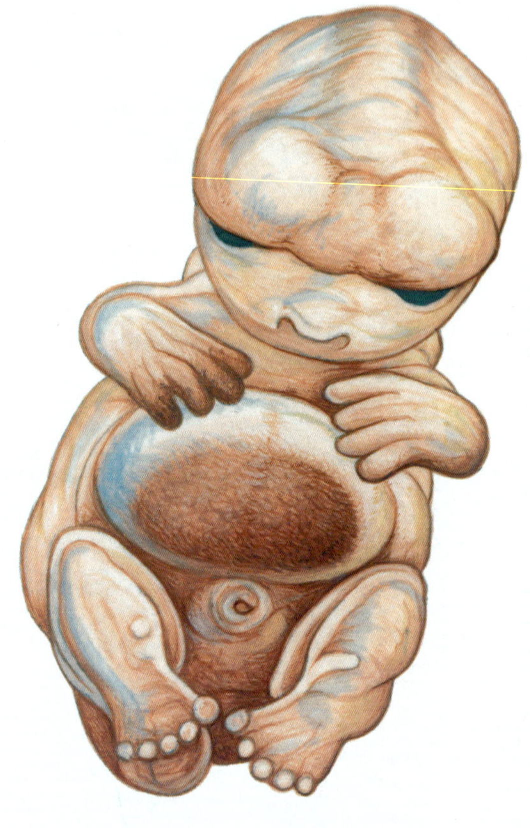

At seven weeks, the embryos of a dolphin (*left*) and a human (*right*) are remarkably similar, revealing much about the evolutionary relationship between the two mammalian species.

Modern Methods of Taxonomy

Linnaeus and many scientists of his time classified organisms solely based on physical characteristics, or morphology. Since Linnaeus, scientists have discovered additional useful tools for looking for relationships between organisms. Some scientists compare how different animals develop before they are born. The

A baby crocodile hatches (*top*). A steppe eagle chick rests in a nest (*bottom*). The fact that reptiles and birds both hatch from eggs suggests that the two groups shared a common ancestor at some point in the distant past.

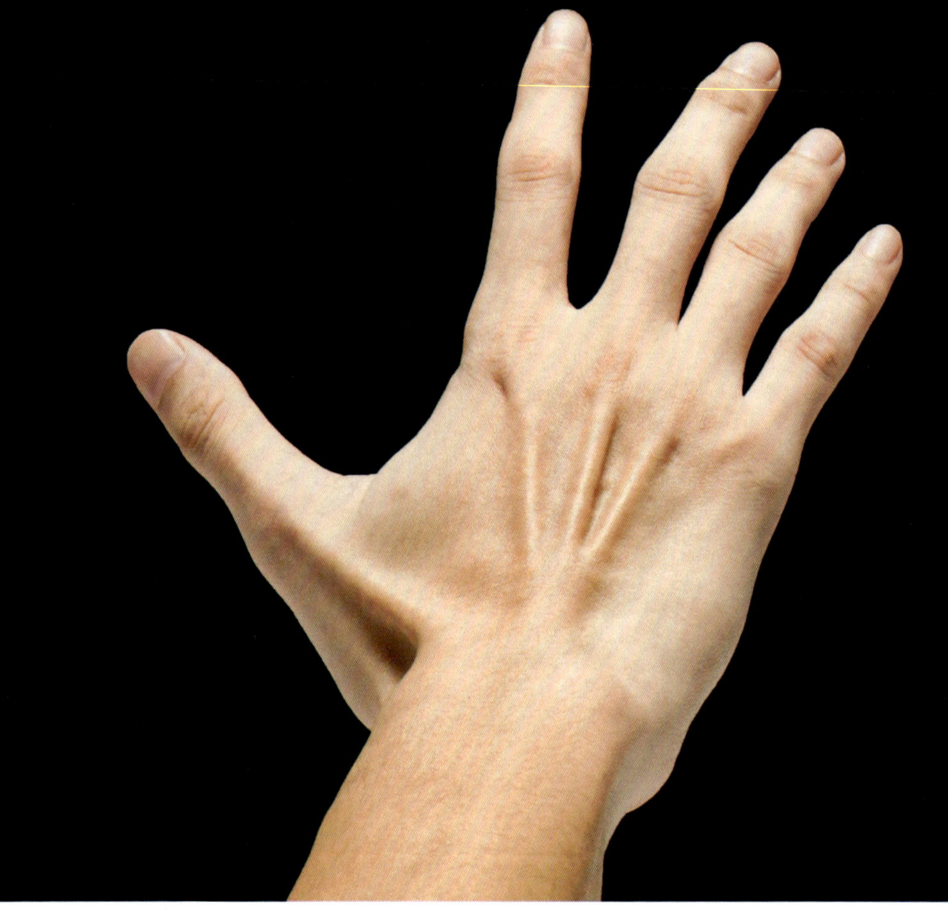

science of embryology has revealed relationships that were not obvious just from looking at physical characteristics of animals. For example, the blue whale, which is a mammal, and the rattlesnake, which is a reptile, both have similar protective sacs that surround their embryos. The crocodile and the eagle both lay eggs with thick shells. Each case suggests that the organisms share a common ancestor.

Taxonomists have always looked for homologous characters. Homologous characters are traits that two different species share because they have a common ancestor. For example, humans and bats both have five digits at the end of their forelimbs. These digits form fingers in humans. In bats, the five digits form their wing bones. This is called homology. Deciding which homologous characters can be used to separate different groups and show relationships can be tricky.

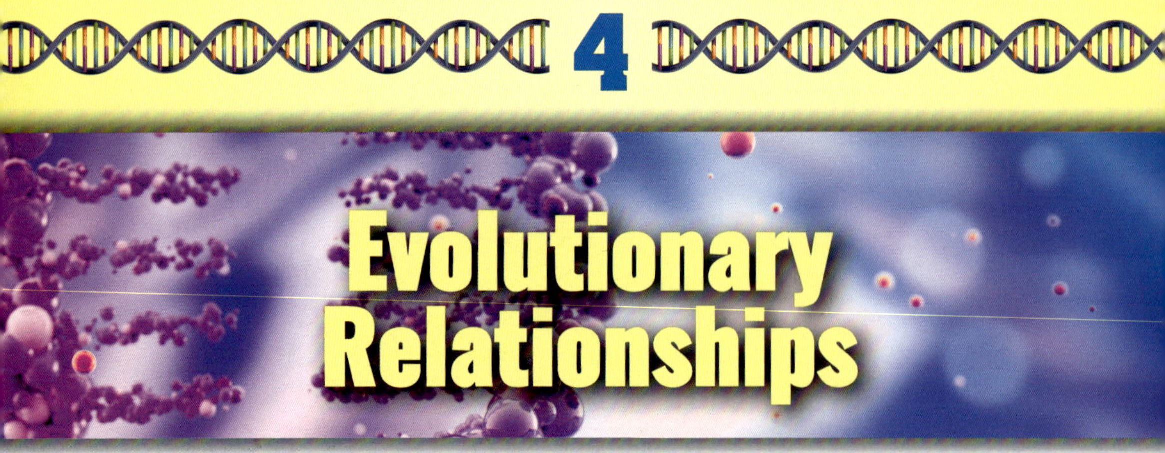

4

Evolutionary Relationships

To understand how organisms have evolved into different species, scientists evaluate inheritable traits. Observable genetic traits include morphology as well as specific DNA sequences. Based on the similarities and differences seen between species, scientists construct a phylogeny, or phylogenetic tree. A phylogenetic tree is a branching diagram that shows the inferred evolutionary relationships between living things.

Charles Darwin

Perhaps the best-known scientist when it comes to evolution is Charles Darwin (1809–1882). As a child, Darwin lived in the English countryside. Young Darwin was interested in nature and science. In his late teens, Darwin studied medicine. But, unlike many other famous taxonomists before him, Darwin did not become a doctor. Despite Darwin's curiosity about the natural world and his enjoyment of plant and animal studies, medical procedures made him queasy. Darwin quit medical school after two years of study.

Charles Darwin is probably best known for his theory of evolution through natural selection.

After Darwin dropped out of medical school, Darwin's father decided that Darwin should be a clergyman. Darwin returned to the university to finish a degree. Again, he was drawn to natural history. He took courses on religion but also took more courses in botany and zoology. When Darwin was not studying, he would often spend his free time collecting beetles.

After Darwin finished his degree, a botany professor, John Henslow, recommended that Darwin go on an upcoming ocean voyage with Captain Robert Fitzroy. who was looking for a naturalist to collect and describe plants and animals on an exploration trip to South America for the British Royal Navy.

The H.M.S. *Beagle* set sail from England in December 1831, returning to England almost five years later. During the trip, Darwin wrote detailed notes and drew sketches of the organisms he encountered. He also collected many plant, animal, and mineral specimens. Years later, Darwin used his observations from his trip to come up with his theory of evolution by natural selection.

The Theory of Evolution

Darwin is often called the father of evolution. In truth, Darwin was not the first person to suggest that different species descended from common ancestors. Darwin and another scientist, Alfred Russel Wallace (1823–1913), working independently, each made the major step of explaining what caused evolution. Both Darwin and Wallace pointed out that the organisms best adapted to their surroundings would survive and pass on their traits to their offspring. Darwin called this mechanism "natural selection," which became known as survival of the fittest. Darwin's name became forever attached to these ideas shortly thereafter when he published his theory of evolution by natural selection in 1859 in his hugely influential book *On the Origin of Species.*

A species is a group of organisms that is able to breed together to produce offspring that also live and reproduce. On the *Beagle* trip, Darwin noticed that many similar species had slight differences. He surmised that their differences helped them succeed in their own habitats. For example, on the remote Galapagos Islands, he noticed various species of finches had differently shaped beaks. These islands were far too distant for much finch migration from the mainland. In addition, the various islands were quite far apart from each other. In fact, Darwin suspected that the finches on each island probably stayed on that island permanently.

One major difference between the islands was the types of food available to the finches. On one island, the finches ate insects and had narrow, sharp beaks. On another island, where the finches ate more larvae and buds, the finches' beaks were broad and hooked. There turned out to be thirteen individual species of finches. Each had a slightly differently shaped beak that was best suited for getting at the food most available. Darwin hypothesized that long ago, a single type of finch came to live on all the islands. Perhaps, he said, they were blown from the mainland while flying through a storm. Over many generations, the finches best equipped for each island survived to pass on their traits to their offspring.

Darwin's process of natural selection has several steps. First, Darwin proposed that offspring with advantageous traits such as beaks better suited for eating the available seeds would survive better than other offspring without these traits. Offspring that survive would produce their own offspring. Those offspring inherited the beneficial traits from their successful parents. Different environments lead to different advantageous traits becoming prominent in offspring. Over time, organisms living in diverse environments become distinct enough to develop into different species—they lose the ability to interbreed.

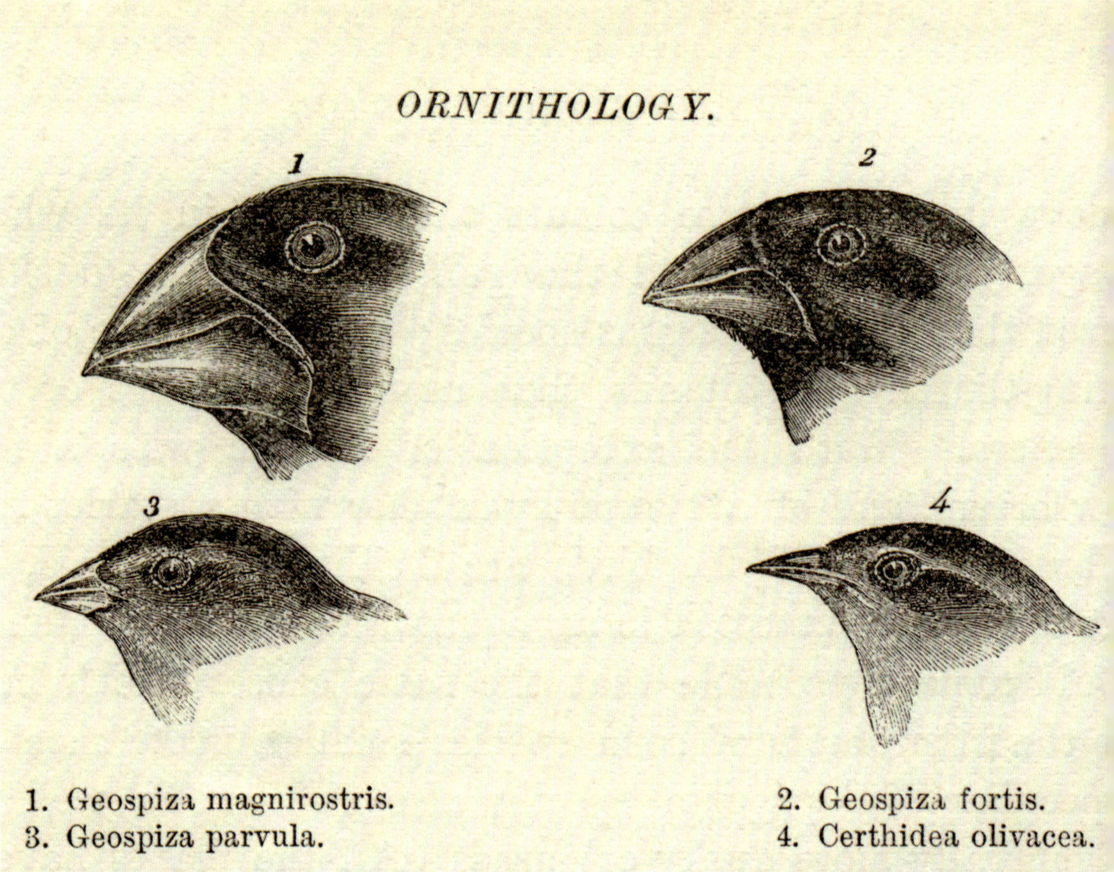

ORNITHOLOGY.

1. Geospiza magnirostris.
3. Geospiza parvula.
2. Geospiza fortis.
4. Certhidea olivacea.

During his voyage through the Galapagos, Darwin observed that finches living on different islands had beaks distinctly shaped for the type of food they could find. The species featured here are the large ground finch (1), the medium ground finch (2), the small tree finch (3), and the warbler finch (4).

The Dawn of Phylogenetics

Darwin described species as branches of a tree. Branches were formed when one common ancestor changed over time into many different species. This idea of new species branching off from common ancestors was new in Darwin's time. Now it is an accepted field of study called phylogenetics.

Phylogenetics is the study of evolutionary relationships between organisms. Before Darwin, systematic scientists looked for homologous traits to help classify organisms into groups. However, they simply thought of the homologous traits as important consistent traits, not as traits that were inherited from common ancestors. Once scientists began using evolutionary relationships, classification made more sense. Relationships between organisms could be sketched out in phylogenetic trees.

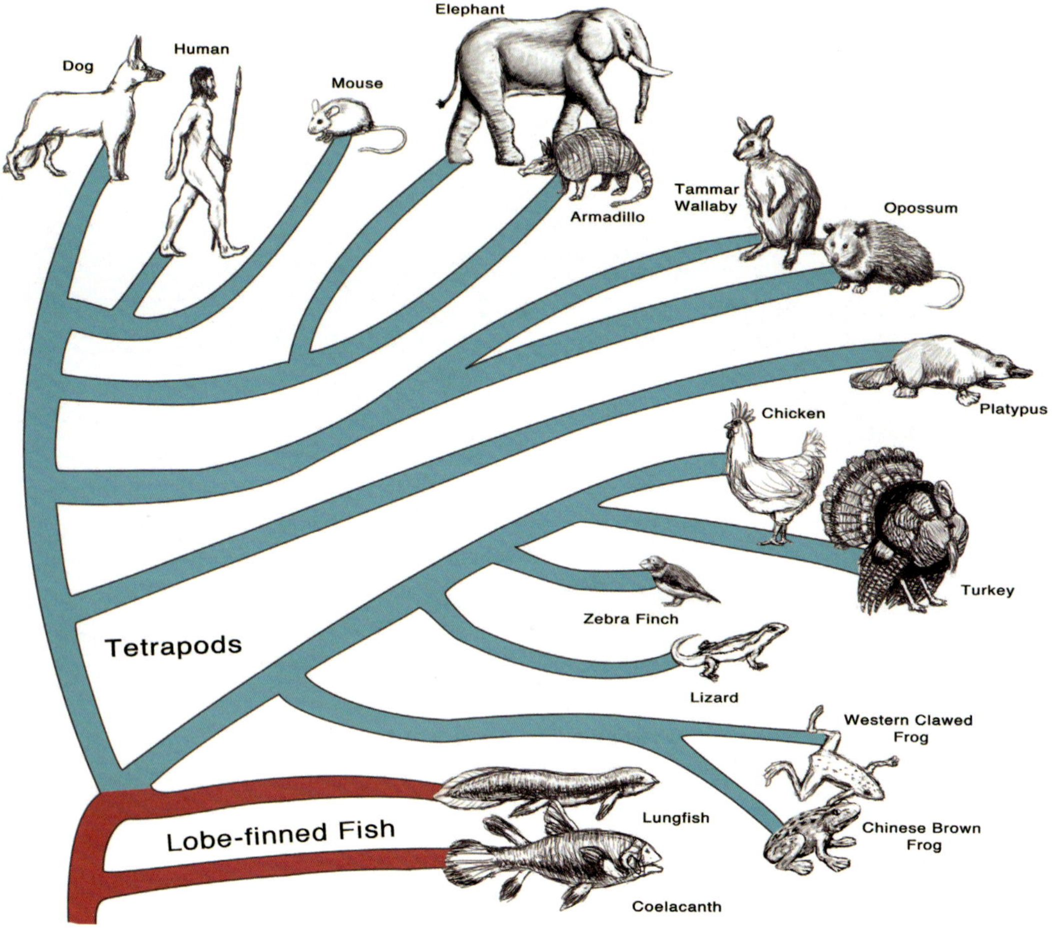

A phylogenetic tree shows how different groups of animals are related to one another.

A phylogenetic tree is similar to a family tree. Family trees have branches that show relationships between individuals in a family. In a family tree, it is easy to see who are the parents of one individual and to see other ancestors such as great-grandparents. Phylogenetic trees show groups instead of individuals.

When scientists correctly classify an organism, they try to find its true place in the phylogenetic tree. Correctly classifying organisms can be a difficult task. The task is easier now, however, than it was before Darwin's theory of evolution by natural selection. Before Darwin, scientists had trouble explaining divergence and convergence. Divergence is the splitting of one species into others. When one species becomes separated into different environments, the groups in unalike environments adapt to become distinct species over time. After Darwin, scientists were able to link differences in similar species to differences in their environments.

Before the theory of evolution by natural selection was accepted, convergence was also particularly confusing to scientists. Convergence is what happens when two or more distantly related species inherit traits that appear similar. In reality, the similar traits are from different ancestors and have evolved separately. The similar species may look alike but they are not closely related. They look alike in some ways because they exist in like environments. In those environments, it is an advantage to have particular traits. Similar traits formed by convergence are known as homoplasies. For example, the duck-billed platypus has a bill that resembles a duck's bill. Ducks and platypuses both live near water and find their food in the water. But a platypus is a mammal and a duck is a bird. Both animals likely evolved bills because they are useful for catching and eating small food items found in the water. However, the duck and platypus inherited their bills from unrelated ancestors.

A Closer Look at Convergence and Parallelism

At first glance, whale sharks (*Rhincodon typus*) and North Atlantic right whales (*Eubalaena glacialis*) might appear to be closely related. They both are large ocean animals that have large blunt heads with big mouths. They have similar coloration: dark gray or brown on the top of their bodies and lighter underneath.

Whale sharks and right whales are both filter feeders with similar diets. They both feed by opening their large mouths and sucking in water. Whale sharks have teeth, but they do not use them. Instead, plankton, small fish, small invertebrates, and fish eggs in the water get stuck on stiff bristle-like structures called gill rakers. Right whales do not have teeth. Instead, they have baleen plates. The baleen plates are similar to the whale shark's gill rakers.

Though whale sharks live in the warm waters of the world and right whales in the colder waters, the ranges of the two species overlap slightly in waters near the Florida coast. Whale sharks and right whales look and act alike because they have adapted to feeding on similar prey in similar environments. But they come from very different lineages. Like other sharks, whale sharks belong to the class Chondrichthyes. Chondrichthyes are cartilaginous fish. Their skeletons are made of cartilage (similar to that on the tip of the human nose). Right whales, on the other hand, belong to the class Mammalia and the order Cetacea. Cetacea includes all whales, dolphins, and porpoises. Cetaceans are more closely related to cows than to whale sharks.

The observation that whale sharks and right whales have similar features passed on from adaptations of different ancestors

Whale sharks (*top*) and right whales (*bottom*) are not as closely related as they appear. Their similarities are a result of adaptations to a similar environment rather than inheritance from a common ancestor.

is a good example of convergence and parallelism. The large size of whale sharks and right whales is useful to both species because few ocean predators will attack huge animals. Plankton is plentiful in most parts of the ocean, so their diet is also suitable for a large animal. Both species come from ancestors that adapted over time to use a sieve-like system to get their food.

As science advanced after Darwin, scientists discovered that many organisms classified in the same groups for morphological reasons also shared common traits that could not be seen. For example, closely related species also share particular DNA sequences.

5

Shared Derived Charactistics

To form a hypothesis about how different species are related, scientists collect and analyze evidence of shared characters. A character is any heritable traits—including physical characteristics, genetic sequences, and behaviors—that can be compared across species.

Conserved Characteristics

Some traits change quickly in species. Others do not. The traits that change quickly are often ones where different forms are beneficial in different environments. For example, all mammals are believed to have descended from an ancestor with five toes or digits. Some mammals such as primates still have five digits on their feet but many, such as horses, do not. Different species of mammals have feet that come in different shapes. The number of digits and the shape of the foot are characteristics that vary in relation to what is best for where a particular mammal species lives and how it moves.

All mammals have hair. Beavers have dense fur. Dolphins are born with a tiny amount of whisker-like hair on their chins that they lose as they grow. But all mammals have hair made of a protein called keratin while modern reptiles, amphibians, fish, and birds do not. This hair on mammals is called a conserved characteristic because it appears on all mammals. Hair on other creatures, such as hairy caterpillars, is not made of keratin. Conserved characteristics do not disappear quickly as species evolve. The fact that these traits last a long time makes these characteristics useful for classifying related organisms.

Cladistics

For a while, scientists continued to struggle to classify living organisms using the evolutionary relationships each organism had to other organisms. One way to discover how and where different species branch off from one another in phylogenetic trees is to use a process called cladistic analysis or cladistics.

A clade is a group made of an ancestor and all of its descendants. The Greek word *clados* means "branch." Cladists look for branching relationships within a selected group of species using shared traits. Some examples of characters that are analyzed are tooth length, beak shape, and brain size. The cladist uses the branching relationships to make logical assumptions about which characters a common ancestor had. The common ancestor's form of the character is called a conserved trait, or a plesiomorphy. The changed form of a character that some newer ancestors have adapted to is called a derived trait, or an apomorphy. The branched diagram created by cladistic analysis of a group of species is called a cladogram.

Cladistic analysis can use physical, molecular, or even behavioral characters. DNA or RNA base sequences are often used in cladistics. When scientists use DNA to construct a cladogram, the shared characters they use are small sections of DNA. They look for sections of the gene code that remain stable

Like all mammals, a beaver's fur (*bottom*) is made from keratin. Insects, such as the hairy caterpillar (*top*), may be covered in tufts of fur, but their bristles are made of chitin, not keratin.

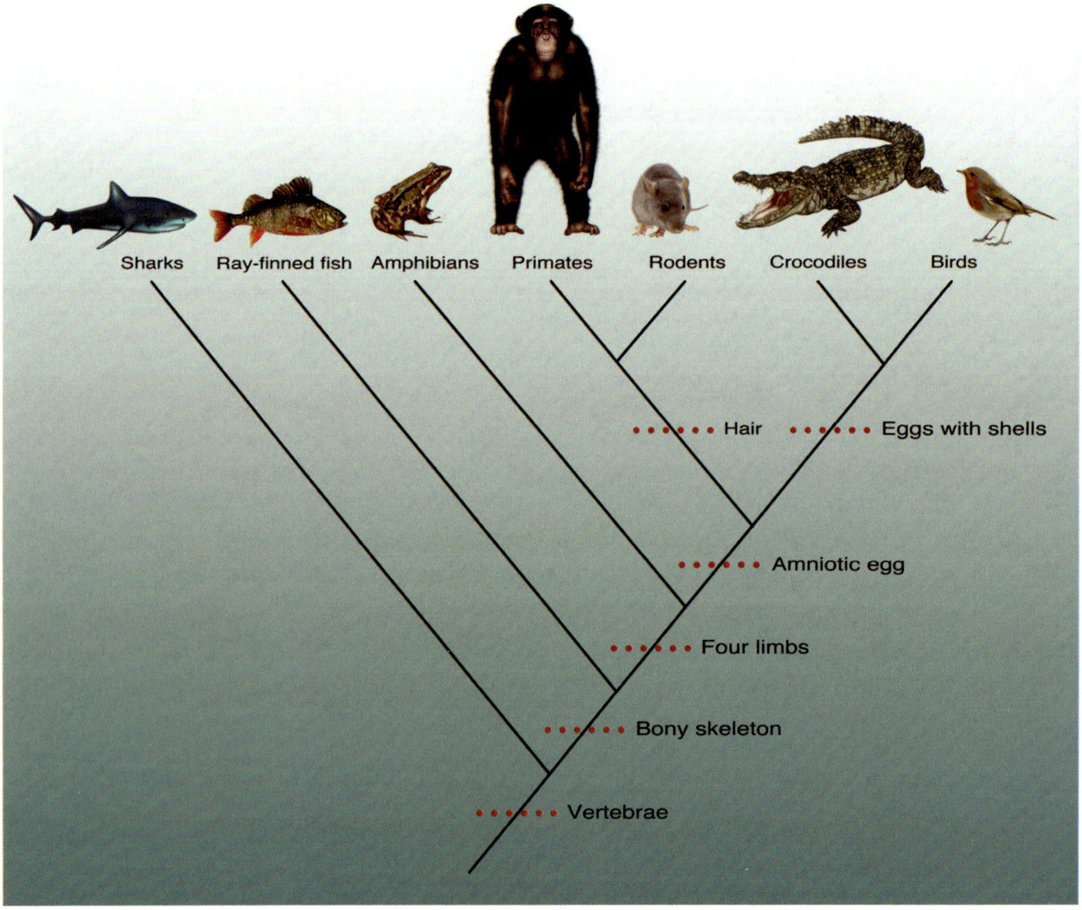

A cladogram shows how groups of animals are related. The dotted red lines show the characteristics that divide the groupings.

and others that change in related organisms. The organisms with the most sections that are the same are often thought to be most closely related.

Cladistics also assumes a clade divides into two new lineages when it branches. Apparent multiple splits simply indicate a need for further study to reduce all divisions into two-way splits. Cladograms show the branching split of two lineages at nodes. Cladistic analysis sounds relatively simple but like all classification techniques, establishing correct relationships between species can be difficult. For example, one species may share an apomorphy with one species and a different apomorphy with another. Cladistics looks for the simplest explanation when trying to decide between different results of analysis. Using the simplest explanation in cladistics is called parsimony. A German entomologist named Willi Hennig (1913–1976) was the first to popularize the use of cladistic analysis. In his writings, Hennig called an ancestor species and its entire descendant species a clade. Eventually, Hennig's methods of looking for evolutionary relationships became known as cladistics.

Hennig was not the first person to suggest using the methods he described, but he was the first person to give clear rules for using cladistics. Hennig said that cladistics should only be used to infer relationships between the species being analyzed. For example, a cladogram was created using characters of different cat species, such as domestic cats, leopards, and lions. The cladogram could only be used to see how those cat species might be related. According to Hennig, the cat species cladogram could not be used to guess how the different cat species are related to domestic dogs because dogs were not included in the analysis.

Hennig also suggested that only synapomorphies could be used to decide which species are most closely related to one another. Synapomorphies are apomorphies that are shared between species. Remember that an apomorphy is a new trait that is different from the trait of a common ancestor. Cladists theorize that if a new form of a trait is found in two different species, it is more likely that they inherited the new trait from the same ancestor than adapted to form the same trait twice.

Cladograms represent nested phylogenies. Nested simply means that the bigger group of the clade is subdivided into smaller groups of related sister groups. Sister groups are two groups that branch off from each other on the cladogram.

A cladogram that shows the order in which different related species branched off from each other is called a rooted cladogram. A cladogram that shows relationships with no chronological order is said to be unrooted.

SCIENCE IS NOT STATIC

Multiple lines of evidence support the clades scientists have divided life into and the phylogenies they have constructed. However, it is unlikely that their work will remain unchanged. Ideally, science is a field of nonstop discovery and, when new evidence surfaces, good scientists reevaluate their hypotheses and conclusions. As new species are discovered or new evidence about old species comes to light, it is likely that branches on the phylogenetic tree will need to be rearranged. This revision does not mean scientists have failed to do their jobs. Nor does it mean they are doing their jobs poorly. It simply means they are doing science.

Cladistics Versus Traditional Taxonomy

Cladistics sometimes clashes with the classification system developed by traditional taxonomists. For example, for a long time all snakes, lizards, crocodiles, and other scaly land animals have belonged in a class called Reptilia. Robins, blue jays, and pink flamingos belong to a class called Aves. Dogs, bears, and people belong to a class called Mammalia. Cladists disagree with this way of classification. If representative species from each group were analyzed on a rooted cladogram, the cladogram would show that all three groups shared a common ancestor. A saltwater crocodile, however, would be evolutionarily closer to this common ancestor than a pink flamingo because the crocodile and the common ancestor share lots of characteristics. A German shepherd, which shares the fewest common characteristics, would be evolutionarily the furthest away from the common ancestor.

At one time, taxonomists classified humans into their own family, Hominidae. Consequently, humans and their extinct relatives, such as *Australopithecus* and *Neanderthal* were often called hominids. Other primates, called the great apes, which include chimpanzees, gorillas, and orangutans, were placed in an entirely different family called Pongidae. These family groupings were made primarily based on physical characteristics. Cladistic analysis, however, shows orangutans, gorillas, chimpanzees, and humans are actually quite closely related. Genetic analysis has confirmed that gorillas and chimpanzees are more closely related to humans than they are to orangutans.

Because of these genetic discoveries, the Hominidae family now includes orangutans, gorillas, chimpanzees, and humans. The subfamily Homininae excludes orangutans and is, therefore, made up of gorillas, chimpanzees, and humans. The subfamily

Genetic analysis has shown that gorillas (*bottom*) are more closely related to humans than they are to orangutans (*top*).

Homininae is further divided into the tribe Hominini, which includes humans and all of their extinct ancestors. Because of the tribe name, humans are now often referred to as hominins rather than hominids. It is not considered incorrect to call humans hominids, however. They still belong to the family Hominidae. But the term "hominin" is more precise.

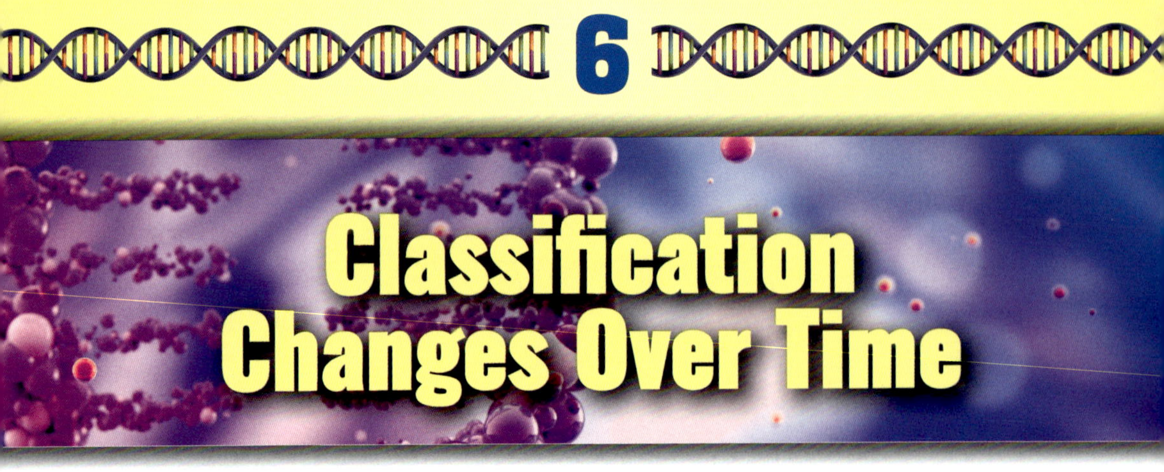

The human family is not the only way taxonomy has changed over time. As new information is discovered, science must change and, just as species evolve, so does the science of classification.

Three Kingdoms

For more than two thousand years, scientists classified living creatures into two groups called plants and animals. Plants are green and grow from the ground. Their cells have a thick wall around them. Animals are often visible, noisy, and usually motile, meaning they can move about. The differences seem clear enough. Since the 1600s and the invention of microscopes, scientists have learned even more about the difference between animals and plants. A thin membrane with no thick cell wall surrounds the cells of animals. Scientists called these large groups kingdoms and the idea of kingdoms is still very important.

The microscopic animalcules that Dutch naturalist Antoni van Leeuwenhoek (1632–1723) had discovered, some in his own bodily waste, were very simple creatures. Still, some photosynthesized, like plants, and some swam around, powered by tiny tails called flagella. Scientists used these observations to classify them as plants or animals. Other microscopic organisms, however, foiled

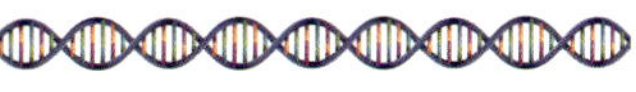

Most species of euglena have both plant and animal characteristics, which made it very difficult for early taxonomists to classify them.

scientists' efforts to classify them. The euglena, a single-celled creature discovered by Leeuwenhoek, was motile and had a primitive eyespot. But it also had the ability to photosynthesize.

In 1866 a German scientist named Ernst Haeckel (1834–1919) suggested a third kingdom, called Protista. Haeckel was a firm believer in Darwin's theory of evolution. He believed that very similar organisms, such as dogs and wolves, came from a relatively recent common ancestor. He reasoned that very different organisms, like dogs and houseflies, had a common ancestor much longer ago. The common ancestor of dogs and common bacteria would have existed even longer ago still. Haeckel hypothesized that these new microscopic organisms that Leeuwenhoek had described might be the common ancestor of all plants and animals. These microorganisms were so small, so simple, and so completely different from other animals and plants that they could be the most ancient common ancestors of all life.

Haeckel noticed that the microorganisms were similar to both plants and animals in some ways. If these creatures were the common ancestors of all organisms, he pointed out, then they could not be called a plant or an animal. So Haeckel suggested that these tiny living creatures should be placed into their own kingdom.

Haeckel's creation of a third kingdom based on how creatures were related signaled a tremendous change in classification. Not only were people used to just two kingdoms, but until Haeckel's time, scientists grouped life based on an organism's appearance or behavior. Tigers, lions, and cheetahs all have a furry, slinky appearance and all were carnivorous. They are easily grouped as animals, particularly as cats. Fir trees, hemlock trees, and blue spruce trees all have needles and cones. They are easily classified as pines: soft, woody plants. These living organisms are easily grouped by their appearances and behaviors.

Four and Five Kingdoms

Microscopes became more powerful through the early part of the twentieth century. Scientists continued to study microorganisms and began to realize just how different all these protists were from each other. Perhaps they should not all be in the same kingdom.

In 1956 a scientist named Herbert Copeland (1902–1968) tried to solve this problem by splitting Haeckel's kingdom Protista into two groups. He put the prokaryotes, which had no nucleus, in a new kingdom he called Mychota. He put the eukaryotes, with their complex cell structure, many of them multicellular, in a group he called Protoctista. This group contained red algae, dinoflagellates, fungi, and single-celled creatures with a nucleus.

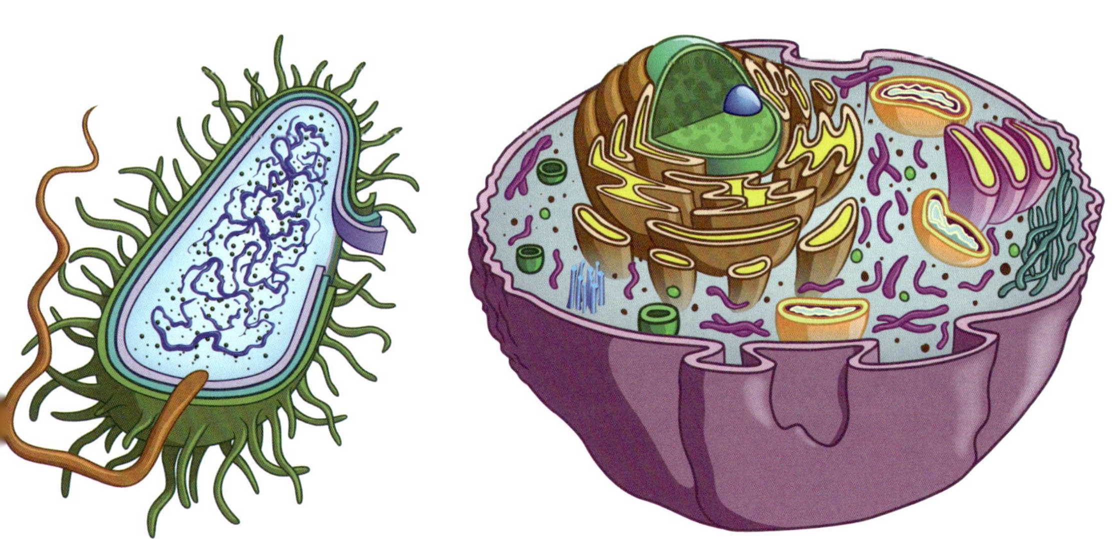

Prokaryotes (*left*) do not have a nucleus or other membrane-bound structures like eukaryotes (*right*) do.

Copeland was just one of a large group of scientists who realized that having a nucleus and complex cell structure was an enormous step in evolution. Bacteria clearly were very simple. They had only a cell wall, cytoplasm, which is everything contained within the plasma membrane cell, and sometimes one or more whiplike structures, called flagella, that served to move them around. Bacteria have fewer specialized structures within the cell, only photosynthetic membrane systems and gas vesicles.

It was not long before scientists saw that another group of organisms was different enough to deserve its own kingdom. Fungi had always been included in the plant kingdom or, in Copeland's system, Protoctista. They grow out of the ground or on other materials and, like plants, do not move around as animals do.

In 1959 American biologist Robert Whittaker (1924–1980) proposed that fungi are very different from plants. Whittaker studied the ecology of fungi. He pointed out that fungi hold a very different place in the food chain. Plants are called producers. They use chlorophyll to trap the energy of sunlight and produce sugar. Trees, bushes, and grasses all use broad green leaves to capture the energy of sunlight, produce food, and grow. Plants are then eaten by many other life-forms. Nearly all Earth's energy comes from the sun and forms the base of the food chain.

Fungi hold a completely different place on the food chain. Fungi break down, or digest, other organisms for their food. When food goes bad or gets moldy, it is usually a fungus growing on the food, digesting it. The mold absorbs the nutrients and uses them for energy it needs to live and grow. Fungi are known as nature's recyclers.

By recognizing Fungi as a separate kingdom, Whittaker suggested that there were five kingdoms: Plante, Animalia,

Mushrooms are the reproductive structures of a fungus.

Monera, Protista, and Fungi. Whittaker's five kingdoms arrangement quickly became accepted. Changes to the tree of life did not stop, however.

New Technologies and New Divisions

Just as the invention of the microscope led to new discoveries, new technologies again played a role in a major advance. By the early 1970s, scientists could sequence, or read the order of, DNA and RNA bases. These genetic molecules make up the instructions that an organism needs to live, grow, and reproduce. Parts of the DNA molecule are called genes. Some genes can be found in all organisms. Genes change bit by bit as populations evolve. Close relatives, such as humans and chimpanzees, are very genetically similar. The more distant relatives, such as humans and slime mold, are much less genetically similar.

In the early 1970s, Carl R. Woese (1928–2012), an American molecular biologist, was studying bacterial RNA. Woese and his team compared one particular gene found in a mouse, in duckweed, in yeast, and in a few species of bacteria. The results proved to be historic.

Woese and his team confirmed that the mouse, the duckweed, and the yeast were closely related—surprisingly close, considering how different the organisms look to the naked eye. The real surprise, however, came when Woese examined the relationships between the various bacteria. Two of the species of bacteria, called methanogens because they produce methane, showed that they were very distant relatives of the other two species of bacteria. In fact, the methane producers were so distantly related to the other bacteria that they were actually closer relatives to the mouse, the duckweed, and the yeast. It was almost as if they should be in their own kingdom.

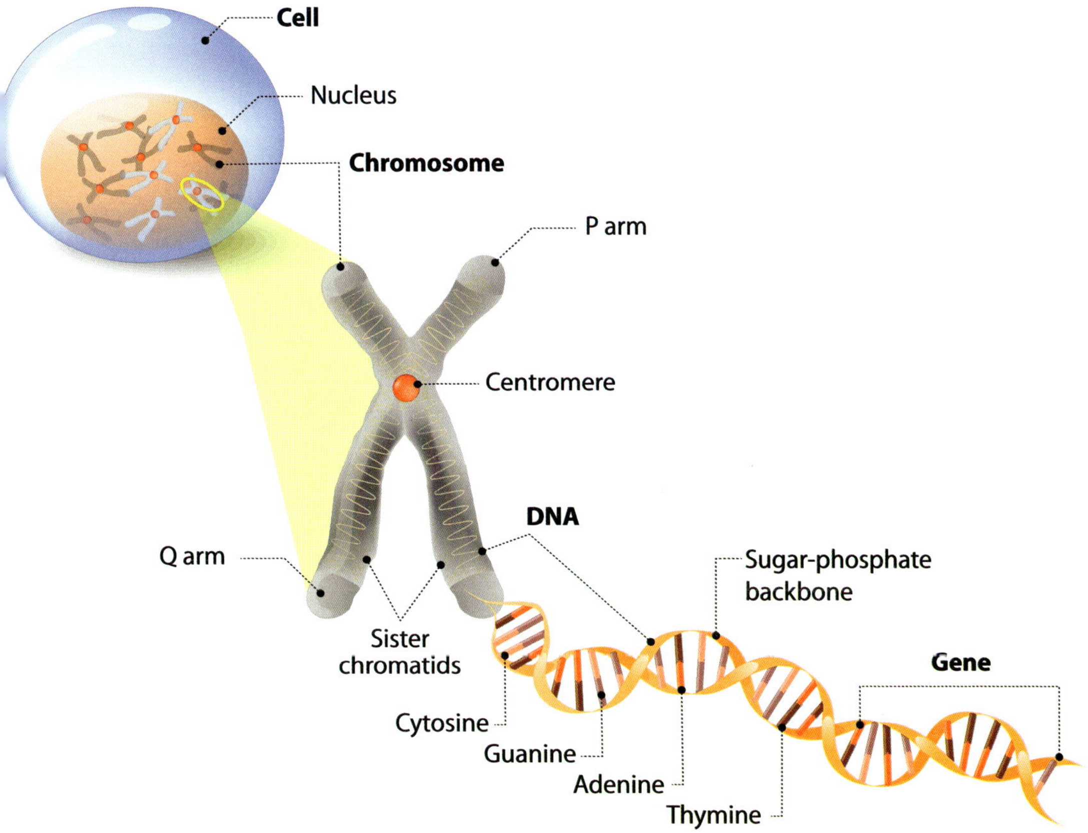

A gene is a section of DNA that contains the instructions for constructing a protein. DNA is condensed into structures called chromosomes, which can be found in the nucleus of most cells.

HIERARCHICAL CLASSIFICATION MADE EASY

Organizing living things into smaller and smaller groups may make a biologist's life easier, but how do they remember which group is bigger than another? People have many ways of remembering the order of things. One way is to make up a mnemonic, or a device for aiding memory. Acronyms are common mnemonics. An acronym is a word made from the first letters (or, sometimes, syllables) of a phrase or a string of words. To remember taxonomic hierarchy of domain, kingdom, phylum, class, order, family, genus, and species, for example, someone might remember the phrase "Do Kids Play Chess or Family Games? Seriously?" The phrase "Do Keep Placing Cake Orders for Good Students" would work, too.

Woese decided to divide the different types of bacteria into two groups called Archaea and Bacteria. But he did not make these groups kingdoms. The two groups were such distant relatives that Woese created a whole new rank above kingdom, called domain.

The domain Bacteria contains many single-celled organisms that people have experience with. The Bacteria species *Escherichia coli*, popularly known as *E. coli*, live in people's bodies and help digestion but sometimes make them sick. The species *Mycobacterium tuberculosis* causes the deadly disease tuberculosis that kills about two million people annually.

The domain Archaea is also made up of single-celled organisms. The Archaea differ from Bacteria in the make up of their cell walls, the complexity of the proteins that direct the copying of their genetic material, and the way they break down food. They are found throughout the world, in the oceans as well as in unusual environments, such as hot springs. Many eat strange foods, such as ammonia or metal ions, instead of using sunlight for energy.

The third domain, Eukarya, is the domain of eukaryotic organisms, which means they have complex cells with a nucleus. This domain includes plants, animals, and fungi as well as protists.

Why Classify?

It has always been the dream of people to learn about the natural world and to name and classify all the new creatures and organisms that are discovered. There are other reasons, however, that accurate classification of organisms is important.

Humans still use many species of plants, fungi, and bacteria for medicine, for improving farming techniques, and to manufacture foods, such as bread, wine, and cheese. But the expanding human

A marine biologist examines a sea urchin in Honduras. The ocean is full of new species waiting to be discovered and classified.

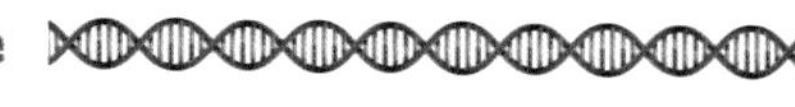

population is changing the planet. Humans are working to prevent those changes from making living things go extinct.

In order for scientists all over the world to understand if a species has ceased to exist or if a new one has been found, they need to have a common language of classification. Taxonomy allows scientists to communicate information about living things without confusion. It allows them to determine how many living things there are on Earth, how diverse they are, and how they closely they are related to one another.

American Cetacean Society. "Killer Whale or Orca." Retrieved November 8, 2017 (http://www.acsonline.org/orca--killer-whale-?).

Annenberg Learner. "Unit 3: Evolution and Phylogenetics." *Rediscovering Biology*. Retrieved November 8, 2017 (https://www.learner.org/courses/biology/units/compev/index.html).

Gee, Henry. *In Search of Deep Time: Beyond the Fossil Record to a New History of Life*. New York, NY: Free Press, 1999.

Grzimek, Bernhard. "Grzimek's Animal Life Encyclopedia: Evolution." Detroit, MI: Gale Cengage Learning, 2011.

Harris, Eugene E. *Ancestors in Our Genome: The New Science of Human Evolution*. New York, NY: Oxford University Press, 2015.

Judd, Wes. "Weirdest Species Names." *Australian Geographic*. March 12, 2014. Retrieved November 10, 2017 (http://www.australiangeographic.com.au/topics/science-environment/2014/03/funniest-species-names).

Manktelow, Mariette. "History of Taxonomy." Uppsala University. Retrieved November 8, 2017 (http://atbi.eu/summerschool/files/summerschool/Manktelow_Syllabus.pdf).

National Cancer Institute. "A Story of Discovery: Natural Compound Helps Treat Breast and Ovarian Cancers" March

31, 2015. Retrieved November 10, 2017 (https://www.cancer. gov/research/progress/discovery/taxol).

National Center for Biotechnology Information. "Genomes." Retrieved November 10, 2017 (https://www.ncbi.nlm.nih.gov/ books/NBK21122/).

National Geographic. "Right Whale." Retrieved November 10, 2017 (http://animals.nationalgeographic.com/animals/ mammals/right-whale.html).

National Geographic. "Whale Shark Profile." Retrieved November 10, 2017. (http://animals.nationalgeographic.com/animals/ fish/whale-shark.html).

Penguin World. "*Aptenodytes.*" Retrieved November 10, 2017 (http://www.penguinworld.com/types/aptenodytes.html).

SeaWorld Parks & Entertainment. "Bottlenose Dolphin." Retrieved November 7, 2017 (https://seaworld.org/en/animal-info/animal-bytes/mammals/bottlenose-dolphin).

SeaWorld Parks & Entertainment. "Monarch Butterfly." Retrieved November 7, 2017 (https://seaworld.org/Animal-Info/Animal-Bytes/Arthropods/Monarch-Butterfly).

Smithsonian Ocean Portal. "North Atlantic Right Whale." National Museum of Natural History. Retrieved November 8, 2017 (http://ocean.si.edu/north-atlantic-right-whale).

University of California Museum of Paleontology. "Understanding Evolution." Retrieved November 6, 2017 (http://evolution. berkeley.edu/evolibrary/home.php).

University of Chicago Press Journals. "A New Estimate of Biodiversity on Earth." *ScienceDaily.* August 30, 2017.

Retrieved November 7, 2017 (https://www.sciencedaily.com/releases/2017/08/170830094326.htm).

University of Virginia. "Phylogenetic Systematics." Retrieved November 8, 2017 (http://www.faculty.virginia.edu/evolutionlabs/Phylogenetics_Page.html).

Wagner, Andreas. *Arrival of the Fittest: Solving Evolution's Greatest Puzzle.* New York, NY: Current, 2014.

Wayman, Erin. "What's in a Name? Hominid Versus Hominin." *Smithsonian.com.* November 16, 2011. Retrieved November 10, 2017 (https://www.smithsonianmag.com/science-nature/whats-in-a-name-hominid-versus-hominin-216054/).

Glossary

apomorphy A derived trait that differs from the ancestral trait, which can be used to separate one group from another.

clade A group made of an ancestor and all of its descendants.

cladistics Classifying organisms into an evolutionary tree based solely on shared characteristics.

cladogram The branched diagram created by cladistic analysis of a group of species.

conserved characteristic A trait that does not disappear quickly as a species evolves.

convergence The evolution of similar traits in two or more species that have evolved separately because of like environments rather than inheritance from a common ancestor.

divergence The splitting of one species into one or more different species due to separation and adaption to different environments.

dorsal nerve cord A hollow cord that develops into the nervous tissue of the brain and spinal cord and is present for at least part of the life cycle of the phylum Chordata.

embryology The study of how animals develop before they are born.

eukaryote An organism whose cell or cells contain nuclei and other complex structures with membranes.

gene A section of DNA that contains the instructions for building a protein.

homology Any trait shared between organisms due to shared ancestry.

homoplasy A similar trait which evolved separately from different ancestors.

microorganism An organism that is microscopic, or invisible to the naked eye, and often single-celled.

morphology The structure and form of an organism.

notochord A flexible support structure that develops into the bone and cartilage of the vertebral column, or backbone, and is present for at least part of the life cycle of the phylum Chordata.

parsimony The assumption that traits of an organism are unlikely to evolve twice and so are more likely to be shared characteristics inherited from a common ancestor.

pharyngeal slits Perforations in the pharynx (throat) wall that are used for filter feeding and that are present for at least part of the life cycle of the phylum Chordata.

phylogenetics The study of evolutionary relationships between organisms.

phylogeny A branching diagram that shows the inferred evolutionary relationships between organisms.

plesiomorphy An ancestral, or conserved, trait.

prokaryote A single-celled microorganism which has a very simple cell structure and no nucleus or other membrane-bound organelles.

species A group of organisms capable of exchanging genetic information and producing live offspring.

synapomorphy A trait shared among groups that came from their common ancestor.

taxonomy The science of classifying living organisms.

Books

Anderson, Margaret J. *Carl Linnaeus: Genius of Classification.* New York, NY: Enslow Publishers, 2015.

Arbuthnott, Gill. *Your Guide to Life on Earth.* New York, NY: Crabtree Publishing Company, 2016.

Currie, Stephen. *The Importance of Evolution Theory.* San Diego, CA: ReferencePoint Press, Inc., 2015.

Green, Jen. *Evolution: Investigating the Origin and Development of Species.* New York, NY: Rosen Central, 2013.

Huddle, Rusty. *Human Evolution.* New York, NY: Britannica Educational Publishing, 2017.

Parker, Steve, ed. *Evolution: The Whole Story.* Richmond Hill, Ontario: Firefly Books, 2015.

Rauf, Don. *Inheritance and Variation of Traits.* New York, NY: Enslow Publishing, 2018.

Websites

American Society of Plant Taxonomists

www.aspt.net
This website has information on the research of taxonomy, systematics, and phylogeny of plants.

The Linnean Society of London

www.linnean.org
The Linnean Society provides educational resources for people to learn more about Carl Linnaeus and taxonomy.

The Willi Hennig Society

www.cladistics.org
The Willi Hennig society promotes the field of phylogenetic systematics.

Index

P

parallelism, 46, 48

parsimony, 53

penguins, 30–33

phylogenetic tree, 38, 43–45, 50, 54

phylogenetics, 43–46

phylum, 25, 29–30, 32, 66

Pinax theatric botnaici, 18

plants, 5, 7, 13, 17–21, 23–24, 26, 29–30, 38, 40, 58–62, 67

plesiomorphy, 50

prokaryote, 61

protists, 61–61, 64, 67

R

Ray, John, 18, 20, 30

Renaissance, 17

reptiles, 11, 35, 50

S

Scala Naturae, 11

scientific names, 23–25

scientific theory, 43

Siegesbeck, Johann, 23

Siegesbeckia, 23

species, 5–6, 9, 13, 17–18, 21, 23–25, 29–32, 37, 38, 40–43, 45–46, 48–50, 53–55, 58, 64, 66–69

synapomorphy, 53–54

Systema Naturae, 26, 28

T

taxonomy definition, 7

Tillandsia, 23

Tillandz, Elias, 23

W

Wallace, Alfred Russel, 40

Whittaker, Robert,

Woese, Carl R., 64